FALLING:
A Memoir in Verse

poems by

Georgia Kreiger

Finishing Line Press
Georgetown, Kentucky

FALLING:
A Memoir in Verse

Copyright © 2016 by Georgia Kreiger
ISBN 978-1-944251-94-9 First Edition
All rights reserved under International and Pan-American Copyright Conventions.
No part of this book may be reproduced in any manner whatsoever without written
permission from the publisher, except in the case of brief quotations embodied in
critical articles and reviews.

ACKNOWLEDGMENTS

Sincere thanks to the following publications in which these poems originally appeared:

Backbone Mountain Review: "Prism," "Not As They Fly," "Breakthrough" (first published as "When Water Pipes Burst at 6 A.M.)
Blue Violin: "Mother Rose"
Burning Word: "Watchers"
Earth's Daughters: "Summer School"
Gloom Cupboard: "Betrayal" (first published as "Matriarchy")
Menopause Review: "Boundaries"
Orange Room: "Snow"

Editor: Christen Kincaid

Cover Art: Jason R. Poole, www.jasonrpoole.com

Author Photo: Georgia Kreiger

Cover Design: Elizabeth Maines

Printed in the USA on acid-free paper.
Order online: www.finishinglinepress.com
also available on amazon.com

Author inquiries and mail orders:
Finishing Line Press
P. O. Box 1626
Georgetown, Kentucky 40324
U. S. A.

Table of Contents

Watchers 1
My mother created the world 2
Mother Rose 3
Heart Condition 5
Winter Pageant 6
With her hard-knocks hands 7
Prism 8
Survivors 9
Prayer 11
Falling 12
Snowflake Creed 13
Mother created secrets 14
Nail Down 15
Mother made the rules 16
Aftermath 17
Unrest 18
Mother set out to teach me 19
Betrayal 20
Snow 21
Not As They Fly 22
Tree Drawings 23
Summer School 25
Boundaries 27
And as I grew 29
Breakthrough 30

For all who have endured childhood traumas and remained silent.

Watchers

Years ago
they cut down
the dead oak
I had watched from my window
to build a house
over there.

So full of crows then,
their dark complacency
among rotting branches,
their blue-black
staring, endless,

the oak's branch tips
extending upward like fingers
of a child reaching
for comfort or answers,
the oily crows
waiting for something.

Years,
and still they watch
from a void over there,
dead oak gone,
a blank sky, but the imagined
imprint smeared
blue and gray,
a child reaching her hand upward
waiting for permission to tell
an awful secret.

My mother created the world.

Mother Rose

Tight-lipped,
more pursed
than a kiss,
like compacted layers
of rage,
it fevered
in the mist
of impending day glow
on the trellis
by the back door.
I passed it
on the way to school,
a bud,
rush of color
like a slap

swelled, surfaced
on my face
where her hand
came down,
because I didn't
stand up straight
enough.
On the school bus
I hid
my stinging cheek
in my palm.

Then it opened,
its yellow core
fringed with pink
cooling to peach,
its name peace,
a small climax
so perfect
I had to call
through the screen door
for her to come
and look.

Heart Condition

Men are fragile,
Mother said, as she and I shoveled
the hard snows that winter.
My father ladled salt
onto the porch steps,
his smooth hands pink with the cold,
his heart falling like the black bird
who dropped down our chimney,
landing in chill ash.
The flail of wings sounded, muted,
through the house. Trapped
in our need not to acknowledge
what was befalling us, we tried to feed
the small bird, but it only thrashed
in protest of its fate. *Fragile*, she said.
Snow asserted its weight
on the weary white of morning.
My father sectioned oranges,
drank stiff tea with honey. And to hear
the flutter of wings like a quick wind,
to know the slow rhythm of snowfall,
I pressed my ear to my father's chest.

Winter Pageant

Fifth-grade girls
who had dance lessons
were picked
to be snowflakes.
Slippered,
brilliant in leotards and net,
masters of fragility and falling
scattering at the bluster
of imagined winds,
gathering center stage,
a swirling sisterhood
of those whose futures
were already awash
in color, buoyant
with prospects.
The other girls: skaters
scuffing the iceless
stage sock-footed
in bulky coats
and mittens.

With her hard-knocks hands and gumption distilled from her elbow grease *and* good-honest-sweat, *Mother made a modest home on a humming street with a car in every driveway.*

Prism

Mother had a talent
for division.

A body, dream,
a white light arrow,
I passed through her

and came out
a shredded memoir,
riding the arc
of her banded river
green-bruise-indigo-violent,

falling toward
a colorless expanse
that was and wasn't me

my hair floating up,
waving a thousand
question marks.

Survivors

One summer,
left to ourselves,
Grandmother and I
pulled weeds.
Sprawled flat
as a Dresden plate
among the lettuces,
or leggy as pea vines,
furred stalks
that bled milk,
graceful wheat-like
plumes. We spared
the ones with tiny
four-petalled
yellow blooms.

The heap we made
began to wither
before we were finished
bending all morning
over beans and chard,
the care of the garden
placed in our hands.

We mounded butter
on our bread,
forgot hand-washing,
our posture and grammar,
the ugliness of the grownup
world—Mother away
for weeks.

Years later,
left at the nursing home,
Grandmother said she wished
she could pull old age,
its winding and choking,
from her like weeds.

Weeds: the things
not wanted.

I remember
their goosenecking
over the onions,
thriving undercover—
spikes of wild mint,
goldenrod, dandelions,
Queen Anne's lace.

Squatters, survivors,
reckless, intrepid,

at her mercy.

Prayer

My father was the rule imposed on the steamy rise of dinner.
His amen was our pistol shot, and when I sat at His table
He read the confessions in my eyes.

On Saturdays I called *My Father, My Father*, and He rained
dimes and candy necklaces down on me. I asked for magic
and He made rosebuds open and the full flowers kiss my cheeks.

At night when the dark windows made me wary,
He came into my room to touch the part of me I could not hide.
My father held our door against intruders. My father was a thief.

Some believe that a cry raised to the unknown is prayer;
others that we should douse our desires in the emptiness that
floats behind our eyes. But my father was a pea coat on the hall tree;

the fall mist rose from His boot prints where He trampled
the buttercups into mud, His stamp upon our garden.
One morning the phone rang and my father was called

to a new garden where mounds of memory threatened
to topple me, and I, a leftover child, skinned
my knees, vaulting the chiseled stones.

I do not weep His absence, nor call *My Father* to a distant star,
for I saw His watch fob, a glimmer between the folds of crepe,
and His ring, its diamond like an eye, on the hand over His heart.

Falling

That winter,
Cousin Payton and I sledded

down the swale across the field
from my house, sledded down

and climbed back up,
our boots crushing the deepening snow,

slid down again into evening, over and over,
racing the cascading shreds of cold.

Our cries, the language of falling,
rose up through the white air.

Sandpaper winds grazed my cheeks
when we left the snow thrashed and ruined.

In the distance, the lit windows of my house
gleamed as we returned our sleds

to the shed out back. *Ten-Year-Old Girl
Raped in Backyard Shed.* No headline there.

Snowflakes blazed on my stiff red coat,
boots clunking along the plowed path back home

where I walked into dusk
with no tongue to cry out to the milk-gray sky.

Snowflake Creed

We embrace the sister attitudes
of fragility and falling.

We are no more than momentary

glimmers on the eyelash
of a child.

We glide fearless down
the milk-gray sky,
though the wind
will know us
with its blustery tongue.

Alit on a fingertip,
we become a tear.

We are
the fingerprints of clouds.

Our hearts are specks
of dust.

Mother created secrets
*   and hid them away*
*   on the highest shelves of her darkest closets*
*   with all her worn-out purses and outdated hats.*

*   Then she told me*
*   to swallow all of the secrets*
*   and hold them inside*
*   because*

      what-others-don't-know-can't-hurt-us.

Nail Down

(Notes for a Poem that Can't Be Written)

He did it, he told me later, because he hated his mother. Cousin Payton said he'd dreamed of nailing her to the hardwood floor, of driving a spike through her womb and listening for the air to rush out as it deflated and shriveled like a leftover birthday balloon. *Products of too much mothering*, they said of all of us kids—*a bad tribe*. Mother should have known, after he took his teenage rage into her shed and smashed all her canning jars with a hammer, the glass splinters ringing their awful music. She should have looked out for me. She should have kept me away from him. He said he was a werewolf, and he would tear me to pieces if I told. I know, I think I know, that my mother knew what happened. He said he hated his mother. He took me instead, he told me, because he needed to crush something easy, and I would never tell. Mother said we keep secrets because *what-people-don't-know-can't-hurt-us*. That winter he took me to the shed. Pounded me out to thin metal, ground my spine into the chill floor. After that I was something, no longer a ten-year-old girl. Something other. When we returned to the house, Mother's eyes met his for just a moment. Part of me is there in the damp dark still.

She knew.

Mother made the rules.

But her rule Things have a way of working out
didn't, which turned our world into a series of sharp
edges and pits full of mumbling,
where even the clearest days were
grayed over by shame.

Aftermath

Not absence exactly,
this loss,
transparent and dull
with its unquenchable ache,
like the cool rush on skin
after a grip releases,
a last warning, don't tell, rises
toward gathering suns,
a shadow retreats,
then nothing.

Not absence exactly,
but an insistent presence
I try to walk off
around this twisted track
of days, this drunken circle;
a presence impalpable,
like a clump of fog
long after dawn
that refuses to
dissipate,
but hangs on
as a ghostly pain may
linger after
an injury heals,
or a small mass
of bad news
on an x-ray
into which I walk,
my inept hands
moving, trying
to re-gather,
to re-shape
this unfounded mist.

Unrest

Sleepless, I imagine they gather my bones out of Mother's shed, while the crows, alert in the trees, cry out in protest. Female, child, missing, yet never missing, lying among the garden tools and saved milk cartons, half buried in sawdust and broken glass. They sift through the clutter trying to find all of me. Skull, finger bones smooth as river pebbles, the gentle arc of a clavicle powdered in grit, radius and ulna, a femur found in the corner, looking like a tree root. The shed lies disheveled as a sleeper awakened by a late night knock at the door, a disturbance in the fragile cycle of waking and sleeping, living and repose. They work my jigsaw bones together on a steel table and coax them to tell my story. But all they can imagine is the vigilant hum of insects, the liquid sigh of a belly melting into the shed floor. Motion, followed by stillness.

Mother set about to teach me:

It takes two to tango *and* You can get used to hanging if you hang long enough *and* If you lie down with dogs, you'll cut off your nose to spite your face.

*But most importantly, she taught me
the* things-you-have-to-do-to-get-by
and all those things-you-don't-talk-about.

Betrayal

I plant daggers
in the pliant ground, my mother,
plant daggers in rows
with a smooth arcing motion.
A dagger is not a seed,
but more like a cell that divides itself
and multiplies itself and spreads
and becomes a house,
rows of houses with fires inside,
a village that stretches to the edge,
the place where the sun disappears.
And out there others, my sisters, are fires—
stoked fires in windows far across fields
and roads, rows of houses, red blazes
like the first rush of blood.

Snow

When reception was poor
on the channel thirteen six o'clock news,
my father called the hissing spatter
of black and white interference snow,
and we sat quietly as meaning dissembled,
watching the white pinpoints of light fall.

It's been years
since I saw him last
at the back door in hunter's camouflage
flushed bright from the cold,
knocking snow from his boots,

and to this day I cannot rearrange
his textured space into a picture.

Not As They Fly—

Straight—along their ruled line
unlike my own unguided march through these woods,

approaching an old man or bare tree
(I can't see clearly enough yet to tell)

that points off to a patch of white
snow or cloud or smoke over the hazy hills.

Not as they fly, but as they haggle over mucked
puddles on this un-etched trail, leaving their haphazard

glyphs in the mud. A poor place
for marching, in a mob of trees,

only the leaves' humid whisper,
nowhere to stretch out a map

to locate myself. Days, memories
branch through these woods

like veins on the back of my hand—not a line,
but the crooked miscellany

of crows, the oily commonness,
the uncommon heaviness of crows,

and in their feathers the gloss and rainbow,
their wings, a map ablaze.

Tree Drawings

Projection, the psych professor said,
giving each of us undergrads
a blank sheet of paper,
to teach us to find the secrets
we draw into trees.
My classmates frowned
at my one slim leaf,
dangling like an elongated
raindrop from a faint line
among the five-fingered
branches I had tried to make
graceful, pleasing.
Looking down on it,
the professor said, *Oh*,
and spoke like a tarot reader
of a traumatic past and present
disorder, as the other students stared.
They had covered their branches
with crayoned green clouds
or well-articulated leaves;
some showed the tree's buried roots
and bony understructure, their drawings
like x-rays—so willing,
they seemed, to reveal
what's underneath.
Some people, the professor explained,
may place a knot hole,
a small circle or blacked-in gap,
on the trunks of their trees,
as if they were timelines and the hole
marked the moment when
the first trauma took place.

At this one student,
who had folded his paper
into an origami swan,
rolled his eyes.
Walking home after class,
I saw the trees standing unwary,
surrendering their slender leaves
to the autumn gusts,
unmoved by my half-buried stories.

Summer School

It took me years to notice
that snow falls year round
at Mother's house.

Summer visits,
ears and toes tingle,
my car fishtailing up her lane.

Her neighbors dance under sprinklers
slurp popsicles and watermelon,
wave sparklers,

while Mother scrapes
the day's accumulation
from her walks,

a white edge
defining her boundaries
the way the horizon marks

the perilous edge
of a flat world.

I make snow monsters
from the drifts of her stories:
how rays from outer space

scramble her chemistry;
the paper girl, sneaking
in her house at night,

mixes up cupboards,
fiddles with the furnace;
how the evening air, so cold,

thickens her blood.

It took me years to wonder
that she could create a world,
how things change when I enter
her private climate,

the way summer storms
cut off suddenly,

when we drive
under a bridge.

I shiver, watching mother
knocking icicles
from her rainspouts,

back braced against
the chill swelter of July.

Boundaries

I prepare for Mother's
yearly visit on my knees,
scrub away crumbs, stains,
a twelve months' residue
of independence, knowing

that everything formless
seeks containment, as spirit
houses itself in flesh
and spilled water gathers
in low spots on the floor.

As always, she makes tea,
turning water to garnet
in the pot, hand-rinsing
and wiping cups while
I look for the honey
I've somehow misplaced.
And I am water,
formless as trust,
and her words, cups.
I feel their hard slippery
boundaries hug tight.

They are the sticks
and stones that break, or build

as God did when he spoke
to the deep and life welled up,
spilling into the perfect molds
of his words,

creating that pull, like gravity,
toward those who would define us.
We reach to the depths
and rims of their words
the way ocean rises and strains
to touch the moon.

*And as I grew,
those secrets rumbled around in their shut-up place,
the muffled thunder of what cannot
(what must) be told.*

Breakthrough
(When water pipes burst at 6 a.m.)

This morning
I wake to water
sluicing through floorboards,
that first dim awareness
of a breakthrough,
and the realization
that for so long now
I have been waiting for a miracle—
that longing inhabits emptiness,
bending the rigid space
between wounding and healing
the way mystics
bend spoons
with one unyielding
thought.

There is a longing so urgent
it can pull other worlds
through walls
the way water
importunes itself
through rock
or old pipes.

Wringing wet towels
on my knees,
I hope they unwound
Lazarus swiftly
as he splashed,
foamy, furious,
through the barred gate
back to this world,

gushing and bubbling
through narrow spaces
between the strips of cloth.

Daylight leaks through
my shuttered windows,
showing up warped wood,
rusty puddles,
bulging wet wall,

and me still waiting
to feel that first tug
at the bindings.

Georgia Kreiger lived most of her life in the hills of Western Maryland. She raised two daughters and worked in the family business before earning her BA from Frostburg State University and her MA and PhD from West Virginia University. Then, in 2012, she embarked on a new life. She moved to Ann Arbor, Michigan, where she now teaches literature and creative writing at Concordia University—Ann Arbor. She writes poetry and memoir, and her work has appeared in such journals as *PoetryMemoirStory (PMS)*, *Earth's Daughters*, *Outerbridge*, *Poet Lore*, *Maryland Poetry Review*, *Sow's Ear Review*, *Hippocampus Magazine* and *Backbone Mountain Review*.

Kreiger endured a number of childhood traumas as she grew up in a large extended Appalachian family. These are the subjects of the poems in this, her first chapbook. She is currently writing a prose memoir that explores these experiences in greater depth. With her writing, she hopes to reach others who have endured childhood traumas and felt isolated by them. In *Falling*, she portrays the unfortunate events in one child's upbringing. Together the poems convey that child's survival and eventual triumph over her circumstances.

www.ingramcontent.com/pod-product-compliance
Lightning Source LLC
Chambersburg PA
CBHW060225050426
42446CB00013B/3167